Learning to Live with Bipolar Disorder

Learning to Live with Bipolar Disorder

Reflections of living life through trauma and mental illness

Jane McGraham

The Choir Press

ISBN 978-1-909300-32-3

Published by The Choir Press

Contents

Acknowledgements

Writing this book would not have been possible without the support from all of my family and friends, work colleagues, and from all the mental health teams in Chichester, Gloucester, and now Cheltenham and Tewkesbury. There are too many to mention.

Firstly I have to thank my wonderful husband Mike, who has encouraged me to write this book, and who gives me so much love and support. Living with someone who has a mental illness is not easy, and he constantly has to cope with the highs and the lows. I love him dearly.

Secondly, to my stepson and family, who have made my life seem so much more complete. I love you all so much. To my dad, I would not have got through all of these years without you. I love and miss you more than I can say.

Thirdly to my many friends; it is difficult to mention you all, but I want to thank my friends in Chichester, Gloucester and Cheltenham. Thank you for your friendship, kindness, and often wise words.

I would also like to thank everyone at The Choir Press for their help and encouragement during the production of this book.

Lastly thank you to God, who has stood by me however difficult life has become, and I know always will. Without your strength I don't think I would be here today. I realise this is not the same for everyone, but having a faith has carried me through, and I hope always will.

I dedicate this book to all my family and friends, but also to all of you who live with a mental illness. It is not easy, but we are not alone!

Prologue

*When I loved myself enough I started writing
about my life and views because I knew this
was my right and my responsibility.*

Kim McMillen (2001)*

Writing this book is something I have wanted to do for years and several friends asked me when I was going to start but, like so many things, I pushed it to the back of my mind. However, with their encouragement, and attending a workshop called 'Writing for Publication' held by the mental health services where I used to work, as well as feeling secure for the first time with my husband, Mike, I decided it was the right time to write my story. The first four chapters include many traumas, which led to me developing a mental illness. The rest of the book gives an insight of what it is like to live with 'Bipolar', and

*www.myinnerspaceblog.com/2012/01/17/when-i-loved-myself-enough-by-kim-mcmillen

the coping mechanisms that help me to live with the illness. Chapter 9 details the early warning signs which are personal to me. I hope they might be a useful tool for others to write their own.

I wanted to write for two reasons. Firstly, writing about the many traumas and putting them on paper was like writing on balloons and letting them go. Keeping my story inside has no doubt contributed to my mental illness. Secondly, because I want to share what it is like living with a mental illness, how it affects the people around you, and learning to live with it. 'Bipolar', a mood disorder which I explain more about later in the book, is talked about a lot in the media today, so it seemed the right time to write about it. All the names mentioned are pseudonyms to protect people's identities.

My story is in no way unique, there are many people who have suffered abuse and traumas of different types, and 1 in 4 live with a mental illness. Within the first 30 years I experienced many types of abuse and traumas. Some of these were in no way my fault, but others happened because of lifestyle choices. There is nothing that happens in life that doesn't have consequences. I have spent almost 20 years living with these consequences, and trying to cope with mental illness, which I have probably had for most of my life. I have developed a resilience which helps me overcome many challenges, and has made me a stronger and hopefully wiser individual.

Living in my Glass Box
Jane McGraham (2011)

Living in my glass box is a strange place to be.
I can see in, but no one knows the glass exists.
Sometimes the glass ceiling and the walls disappear, then
everything appears normal, whatever normal is;
but it's like walking on a tightrope, suddenly you fall off and
the world again is a strange place.
When the ceiling is covered, and the walls are down, the
depression has come, bringing darkness all around.
There appears no way out, and the anxiety creeps up, like smoke
from the floor, and it suffocates every part of your being.
At these times there appears no hope, no way out.
Every job, however small, even breathing appears too much,
but in my glass box no one knows.
They somehow see the happy face, the face
that manages to say, 'It's OK', but in reality it's not.

*'To be sure', wrote Hugo Wolf, 'I appear at times
merry and in good heart, talk too, before others quite
reasonably, and it looks as if I felt, too, God knows how
well within my skin. Yet the soul maintains its deathly
sleep and the heart bleeds from a thousand wounds.'**

Sometimes the glass walls are up and the ceiling
suddenly opens.
It's like being rocketed into space. Life seems wonderful.
Why sleep when there's so much to do?
Ideas come so quickly and race around a track in my head.
It's like being on a 'Waltzer' at the fair, going round and round,
faster and faster, with the wind blowing in your face.

Nothing is impossible, or too small.
I can be a doctor, climb Mount Everest, and travel
around the world.
I want an expensive holiday; buy all the nice clothes I see.
I want to laugh out loud, skip and run. I love this feeling
however mad it is; but then the thoughts become too fast.

Nothing is clear, and I can't slow down.
And then the inevitable drop. It's like falling down a well.
If I'm lucky I hold on to the side and don't drop too far.
I crawl/pull myself to the top and manage to live my
life just like anyone else. You just never know what
will happen next.
It certainly isn't boring living in my glass box.

*From *An Unquiet Mind: A memoir of moods and madness* by Kay
Redfield Jamison, Picador, 1996.

CHAPTER ONE

Jane the Dauntless

I was born in the swinging sixties. For many the sixties was about rock and roll, whereas others continued to live with the hardships from the fifties. The year I was born, 1962, the Cuban missile crisis ended peacefully, which everyone was relieved about, as people feared a nuclear war. My birth mother had me just before her 19th birthday.

Throughout the last 48 years I have been told three different accounts of what happened when I was born: firstly from my adoptive parents, secondly from social services, and lastly from my birth mother, in written form. I have two letters and a photograph, but I haven't been able to talk to her, as she finds that period in her life too distressing to talk about. I respect this, as I know she did not want to give me up for adoption, but circumstances dictated she had no choice. Women were not meant to have a child out of wedlock, and from what she says, her father wanted me 'tided away'.

After a few months in foster care I was adopted by a

couple in their early forties who had been unable to have children. Dad was a school teacher in a small village in Oxfordshire, before taking up a post as college lecturer in Gloucestershire. Mum, having left school, worked as a nursing auxiliary in a hospital, and then as a secretary, but to my knowledge she did not work again after they had adopted me. Up until she died in 1997 I learnt very little about her, as she revealed very little about herself.

I knew her father left the family for another woman, and my mother helped to bring up her two sisters in Sheffield. Although both sisters grew up to be laid back and kind hearted, Mum became bitter, angry and jealous, all of which made for an unhappy marriage. In contrast Dad had only one brother, and was brought up in a very loving home in North Wales. Although his father died young, his mother, my Nine (Welsh for grandmother), lived into her eighties. She was the only grandparent I knew, but as she lived so far away, and died when I was very young, I have very few memories of her.

From what I'm told she adored me, but was rarely allowed to pick me up when we visited. If she did Mum would quickly snatch me back. What she was afraid of I'm unsure. When Nine died, Dad thought Mum must have been relieved, as we seldom visited

Wales after this. Dad told me she found the Welsh difficult, believing they did not accept her. In truth she was often not a likeable person, giving way to bouts of anger towards whoever was in her way. This included Dad and me.

Dad was one of the kindest, most humble men I have ever met, but he was also weak, finding it hard to stand up for himself. I doted on him, not wanting to leave his side. This was largely because I was terrified of Mum. When she lost her temper it was easy to believe she wanted you dead. I was told that when I was very young she would get me up in the middle of the night, bring me downstairs and demand I listen to the arguments my parents were having. I can remember many many times I wished I lived with another family, but never without Dad.

From an early age I learnt that to survive I had to be 'good'. Of course no child can be perfect, and so Mum would continually lose her temper. If I wanted a friend for tea, or to go to a friend's house, I had to be good. If I didn't meet her standards I was not allowed to see my friends.

Dad would try to stick up for me, but this resulted in bigger rows that could last for days; it was easier to be quiet. I have many memories of these rows. Mum would lose her temper over the smallest thing and would scream at Dad because he put the plate in the wrong cupboard, or didn't put the cheese on the right shelf. She would take herself to bed for days after screaming at us.

On one occasion the arguments were so bad, I screamed at her 'Perhaps you should never have adopted me.' I honestly believed I wasn't wanted, and it would be better if I had not been born. Following this row I sat under a tree in a field opposite our home, and something inside me died.

Dad came out and took me to see *Jesus Christ Superstar* at our local cinema. I remember it clearly because I wondered if Jesus loved me, but how could he when I felt so unlovable. When we returned most of my toys, including my doll's house, were outside the front door. I felt numb, and yet inside I was desperately hurting. As Dad pulled down the garage door, I turned to him and said, 'I wish she were dead.' He replied, 'Don't say that, darling,' but it was how I felt.

One Christmas we had finished our dinner, and Dad suggested I watch some television whilst they cleared up. Mum flew at him for letting me watch television. She threw plates in his direction, and another frightening argument began. I sat looking outside the window, and saw a family walking by. The little girl was pushing her new doll's pram beside her mum. They were laughing, and the child had hold of her mum's hand. I remember wishing I lived with them. Of course no one knows what goes on in other families, but to me they appeared to be what a family should be.

At primary school I struggled physically and emotionally to keep up. My parents had been told by doctors that I had 'mild spasticity', resulting from a difficult birth. I struggled to walk and hold a pen, and found reading, writing and maths extremely difficult.

At the age of 5 I couldn't stand up on my own, which caused difficulties at my first school sports day when I was put in the sack race. At the start of the race we all had to lie down in our sacks, ready to stand and jump to the finish line. I was so excited to be in the race, as all the other races were not suitable for me. When the whistle blew the teacher forgot to lift me to my feet. By the time she remembered, the race was over. Apparently I just laughed which I always managed to do, at least on the outside.

It was for reasons like this, my Dad named me 'Jane the Dauntless'. He said that no matter what happened to me I would smile or laugh. In truth I was burying everything inside. I also believed that if I smiled everyone would believe everything was all right. I was desperate to please, especially my parents. It was at this time I began to hear voices in my head, both good and bad. The bad voices would laugh at me, telling me what a horrible person I was, and getting me to do certain things, such as look under the bed, or in a cupboard so many times; if I didn't bad things would happen to me. These voices were not the same as the negative thoughts in my head. They were voices that made me turn my head to look round, to see where they were in the room.

I believed men and women camped outside my bedroom window and had eyes and cameras everywhere, including in the pictures on my bedroom walls. I became very paranoid. I only felt safe around other people, but not when I was on my own with Mum. The good voices would fight on my behalf. They didn't have cameras but somehow just knew what was going on. One in particular, whom I called 'Diggy', became my one true friend. I would talk to him constantly.

On one occasion when Dad saw me rocking and talking to Diggy, who he perceived to be myself, he said, 'Don't do that or they will lock you up.' I did not know exactly who 'they' were, but the thought of being locked away and separated from him was enough for me not to tell anyone from that day what was happening to me.

I was a terrified child, but I didn't cry and began living in what I called 'my glass box'. A box that no one else can see. To the outside world I was Jane the dauntless, but inside I was a confused, terrified and deeply lonely child. I couldn't risk letting others know how I felt, somehow I had to survive.

If Dad went to a meeting in the evening I would lock myself in the bathroom, terrified of being on my own with Mum. If I lay in bed, I would always face the door so I could see the door opening as it was less frightening if I saw her come in.

She would climb into bed with me, or take me into her bed and do things I didn't want her to do, including blowing loudly in my ears. She would then laugh. I both hated and loved her, and could not understand why she treated me this way. I was too frightened to tell Dad, because I believed everything must be my fault.

When Dad and I eventually talked about it when I was in my late thirties, he admitted he was not surprised, and yet with him she had been frigid. In all the years together they had only had sexual relations a handful of times. It was only when I met my husband that I relaxed enough not to face the door any more, but when I stay in Dad's bungalow I am still very aware of the bedroom door, and wake several times during the night, thinking Mum will walk in the door.

It is an irrational thought, but the feelings/ emotions are very real and powerful. If you change the thought, i.e. 'Mum can't hurt you any more because she is no longer here', the anxiety/panic begins to subside. Living with so much panic and anxiety means I am constantly having to work on changing negative thoughts into more positive ones. I will refer to these coping mechanisms later in the book.

CHAPTER TWO

The Early Years

In primary school I found life very confusing. I adored Dad, but why did he let these things happen? Then there was God. Where did he fit into all that was happening to me? For as long as I could remember my parents had asked me to say a prayer out loud that they had created. I would have to get on my knees beside the bed, put my hands together and pray: 'God bless Mummy and Daddy, aunties and uncles, cousins, and Nine, and all my little friends, and make Jane a good girl, for I ask this in Jesus' name, Amen.' Of course I never felt I became a 'good girl'. I was also taken to Sunday School, which I enjoyed because it meant I could spend some time away from home.

Following this I went on to Pathfinders, a group for youngsters in the church, where I had the opportunity to go camping. One night I lay in my tent, and asked Jesus to come into my life. I didn't really know what that meant, but I felt incredibly peaceful. In many ways the leaders were my salvation, showing me the kind of love that I had not known before, and introducing me to a God who they taught only showed love and compassion. During the process of looking for my birth mother in my early thirties, Dad gave me a letter which had been written by the Bishop of Oxford in 1962. Many adoptions were carried out by the Church Society at the time.

Within this letter he writes:

> *We only place children where there is real reason to believe they will have the advantage of a Christian upbringing. Without any attempt to make terms we were satisfied that, with you she would be brought up in the Church to which you belong, and I am sure that this is your intention. I do hope you will be steadfast in this, not only for the child's sake, but for your own. There is nothing that gives greater strength and happiness to the life of a family than being united in the practice of your Christian faith.*

I wonder to this day how they vetted my parents, as my Dad told me on numerous occasions, 'We should never have been allowed to adopt you.' Although I began trusting in a loving God, I couldn't understand why he had allowed me to be adopted by a mother who abused me.

∞∞

On top of this I struggled with feelings of abandonment. I didn't blame my birth parents for giving me up, but inside I felt unwanted. Dad had always told me I was 'special' because they had chosen me, but I didn't feel special. The only time I felt near it, was when I was sat on my Dad's lap or held in his arms. On a Saturday after lunch Dad would read a story called *Lazy Saturday*. I loved this book, and after he had finished reading, he would pretend to go to sleep. I knew he was pretending because he would slightly open one eye, but I didn't care, I would curl up in his arms feeling safe.

I struggled at school trying to make friends, and learning to read and write. Although Dad was a teacher, I was way behind other children my age, which he said was because of the mild spasticity. In the first couple of years I wore callipers on my legs, to try to strengthen them, and had a special device strapped to my right hand and wrist, to help me write. I felt stupid, and was often teased by the other kids. Church and Brownies were the only places where I felt accepted and loved; at least there I wasn't teased.

In my first year of secondary school the arguments at home were daily, and my parents finally separated and went on to divorce. Dad could no longer take the physical and emotional abuse. There were times when Mum would throw knives at him, and hit him with a stick. We tend to believe men do all the abusing, but this is not true.

I don't know why Dad put up with the abuse, but he was soft natured, and he found it hard to fight back. It's difficult to understand unless you live in that situation. I stayed with Dad when she left, and in many ways they were the happiest years of my childhood. I was allowed to see my friends, without any conditions, and for the first time in my life I felt reasonably safe. Dad and I went out a lot, laughed loads, went on our first holiday abroad, and he bought me my first dog, 'Kim', a Border terrier, whom I adored.

However, life was hard as I took on a lot of responsibilities such as cooking and cleaning. Dad found physical jobs hard, as he had a profound limp, which he had had for years. During his youth he had enjoyed rugby and many other sports. Whilst playing rugby, not long after being married, Dad collapsed on the pitch. He was taken to the John Radcliffe Hospital in Oxford, where he was told he had contracted TB, probably from drinking milk straight from a cow. He spent nearly twelve months in hospital, and ended up with six steal pins in one of his hips. As he got older, his hip and leg became more and more painful, and he suffered a great deal.

Despite this he worked hard as a lecturer and I of course had homework, so Dad took on the role of college warden, as well as Dean of Admissions, and we moved into the college where he taught, a wonderful classic old brick building, with loads of corridors and rooms to explore. We had a lovely flat, and having a college cleaner, eating meals at the top table with the students in the college dining room, and spending time with friends, meant life became a lot easier, and I became more sociable.

At school I still struggled, so much so that I was constantly laughed at because I found sport hard. Children called me 'spastic' after they learnt from one teacher I had mild spasticity. I failed exams and had no interest in learning, much to Dad's dismay. He would try to sit me down to teach me, but I didn't want him to be my teacher, I just wanted him to be my dad.

Although life with him was great, several times a year I had to get on a coach and travel alone to the New Forest to stay with Mum. She had moved there to be close to one of her sisters. It felt like being sent to hell, and yet I wanted to see her, she was my mum. The only plus side was when we spent time with my aunt and uncle. Mum's flat was very small, and only had one bedroom, so I had no choice but to share the bed with her. To cope, I took myself to another place.

By the age of 14, although Dad and I were happy, Dad struggled to be on his own. Unbelievably he missed Mum. After several meetings, one at my confirmation, they got back together. I decided that if Dad could forgive her, then I would have to, too. For a few months, living in the college flat, life was OK, but the saying 'a leopard doesn't change its spots' is true. Dad admitted he could not live with or without her, and he hoped she may have changed. These of course were false hopes and he spent the rest of his married life in a very unhappy relationship.

Dad took early retirement and they moved into a bungalow in Lymington in Hampshire. I had moved away from home, but for Dad years of emotional and physical abuse continued. Retiring and moving away meant he had cut himself off from all the other distractions of college life. If he went into town, Mum demanded to know where he had been, and who he had been talking to. On the rare occasions they made friends, she soon made them her enemy. This was so sad, because Dad was so sociable, and loved talking to people. When I went to visit, whilst Mum was in the kitchen, which was her domain, Dad and I would generally chat about life. Mum would suddenly burst through the door, and accuse us of talking about her, which generally wasn't true. She was an angry, jealous, paranoid and bitter woman. I desperately wanted to love her, but often I only felt hatred.

Dad continued to suffer emotionally and was often beaten with a stick. He would talk to a lady at Citizens Advice who gave him leaflets on domestic abuse, and she became a friend to him. I encouraged Dad to leave, but he said he couldn't. In her eighties Mum became very dependent on him, and was scared to have the curtains open in case people were watching. She would also check the door was locked over and over, especially when Dad went out.

I witnessed this on several occasions when they visited me for the day. If Dad went out the door she was terrified. It was very sad to see, and yet whenever I was close to her, or she gave me a kiss or a hug, every part of me cringed. Inside I screamed a silent scream, 'No'.

The last time they visited before she died, I remember standing by Dad's car. Before she got in, Mum took my face in her hands and looked deep into my eyes. I can still see and feel that stare today. I hated it, and yet I grieved for the relationship we had never had. I gave her a hug, but the glass wall was between us. I have asked myself many times if I would have felt differently had I known it was the last time I would see her? Would I have let the glass wall down, so I could hold her closely? I am not sure I could have done anything differently, I had to protect myself.

On the day she died in 1997 she showed Dad affection for the first time in years. In a restaurant in Swindon she simply rested her head on Dad's shoulders and went to sleep. Dad and I kept how we felt to ourselves, but we both had questions that couldn't be answered. What had made his wife, my mother, so bitter and angry, and why had she treated us this way? I went with one of her sisters and my cousin to see her at the undertakers. Dad believed it would help me to accept she had died, and said at last she looked peaceful.

I went into the room feeling terrified, and when I saw her I screamed, perhaps finally letting out the silent scream I had kept inside all my life. I saw no sign of peace, and felt no relief. I ran out of the door, leaving her sister and my cousin to say goodbye. I heard my auntie ask her why she had said those terrible things. I have no idea what 'those' things were.

After they left the room I went back in. I asked her out loud why she had abused Dad and me, and told her I was going to choose to forgive her, but inside I didn't feel forgiveness, just a horrible mix of emotions that I couldn't understand. All I could say is 'It hurts'; in fact I often say that today. It is a pain so deep, it overwhelms me.

I believe forgiveness is a choice that in time releases us from bitterness and hatred. We may not feel it straightaway, but in time we experience more peace than bitterness. This does not take away what the other person has done, but I believe God asks us to forgive for our own good. Mum's death was in many ways the end of a nightmare, but it was a nightmare that would live with me for the rest of my life. I will return to the effect she had on my life later in the book.

CHAPTER THREE

Living Life on a Tightrope

From what I have learnt over the years, abuse of any kind can lead to more abuse. By the age of 15 I had been abused by my mother, a boy in a lane close to where we lived on the way home from church, by a waiter in Spain while on holiday with my Dad, and by a friend of my Dad's, John, that went on for years. Only the last of these was investigated by Social Services years after it had happened. I decided to contact the police when I was in my thirties, because I didn't want him to do to others what he had done to me. It had taken me years to build up the confidence to contact them, and I honestly did not think they would take me seriously after all these years.

I met John when I was still at primary school. He was very good looking, and appeared to be kind. For as long as I remember he had always made a fuss of me, which made me feel good about myself. I'm not sure when the abuse began. It was either when I was still at primary or soon after going to secondary school. A lot of my early memories are still lost, probably after the many traumatic events.

Whilst I was at secondary school and later at technical college John would take me into a room in the college where Dad worked, or sometimes out in the car for a drive in the country. He started by telling me how special I was, and how I could make him very happy. He then went on to abuse me. I could see the expression on his face, how it appeared to make him happy, and he kept stroking my face.

When it was over, he would tell me again how special I was and that I was making him very happy doing this for him. I felt sick and dirty, but I was happy that I was pleasing him. He told me, 'This is our little secret' and that made it seem even more 'special'. The abuse went on for years, up until I left home at 19. I wonder now why I let it go on for so long, but abuse for me was such a normal part of my life.

I was living in Chichester years later when I made the call to the police. A policewoman from child protection visited me from Cheltenham. I was dreading the interview, and was so thankful for having good friends around me, but it was only me that could tell the policewoman what had happened.

It was hard, having to relive everything, but she assured me none of this was my fault.

I felt relieved that I was being taken seriously. She had already made enquiries and found out that John was still working in a place where children visited. This concerned her enough to arrest him and hold him for questioning. She was sure that if he had abused me, he would have abused others.

The police visited my parents after I told them what had happened. It was incredibly hard for Dad to hear, and he wanted to kill him. The police also visited John's ex-wife, who told them she wasn't surprised because he 'loved' young girls. Their marriage had ended because he had had an affair with a much younger woman. John of course denied the abuse. He was released, and the case went to the Crown prosecution.

The policewoman who had interviewed me told me over the phone she knew he was a liar, but a good liar, and the Crown prosecution believed it would be incredibly stressful for me to testify in court, when there was no further evidence that would lead to a prosecution. Although frustrated I agreed, and it was at least healing going through the process.

It was as if I had a sign on my back which said, 'Abuse me'. I left school early with no qualifications. I found lessons incredibly hard, and struggled to concentrate with everything going on in my life. I went on to complete a further education course, and enrolled on a two-year nursery nursing course. Although the abuse continued for some of this time, I at least felt I had achieved something. I was 19 and now engaged to Mark. He had been studying at the college where we lived, and now lived just outside of London. We had been going out for two years, and we travelled by coach to see each other most weekends.

In so many ways it was an unsuitable relationship, as he was several years older than me and had a very serious personality, but I believed I was in love, and so having completed my course, I moved to London to work as a nanny, looking after two boys, aged 2 and 4. It was hard work, but the family treated me well, and I loved living in the centre of London. There was always something to do, and I had no shortage of friends, having been introduced to other nannies.

On a Friday night we would go out to a pub, and then queue to get in to the Hard Rock Café for something to eat at midnight. I loved London and never felt lonely. Mark and I eventually grew apart, and I partied hard, drinking too much, and getting into debt. I lived my life on a high, craving attention from all the wrong people, mostly men, which led me from one disastrous relationship to another. Living your life on a high is wonderful, until you come down again. I didn't realise that I was showing signs of mental illness then.

I moved from one area of London to another, before settling down with a guy called Pete. We shared a flat together on the outskirts of London. He worked locally and I travelled into the centre of London every day to work in an office. For a while life with Pete was good, and I felt settled, but we were paying rent at London prices and he was paying maintenance to his ex-wife for their child. We soon got into debt, and were in trouble with our landlord. Pete had a terrible temper and on one occasion hit me so hard, I was black and blue. Friends begged me not to stay with him, but I desperately wanted to please him.

Although we were both working, being in debt caused so many arguments. Feeling insecure I was prepared to do anything for him, and he would often lay the blame at my feet. Believing it was my responsibility to get some money, and having sold anything that was valuable, one morning in desperation I got dressed up, putting on the shortest skirt I could find, and caught the train into central London. As I sat on the train and then the Tube, I again took myself to the place within me where I was unable to feel any emotional pain. I walked into one of the top London hotels, ordered coffee, and looked at all the well-dressed men coming in and out of the lobby.

I can't imagine what they thought about me, and I hadn't a clue what I was doing there. All I could think was, 'I can't go home without any money.' I must have sat there for a couple of hours, and even travelled up and down in a lift. I felt numb and stupid, but I believed if I could sell myself to someone for lots of money, just the once, it would be the end of all our problems. I could see no other way out. I had the glass box around me, and believed I couldn't get hurt. Sex didn't worry me. It had been so much part of my life, since being a child. I had felt dirty for as long as I could remember, so sitting in the hotel foyer almost felt natural.

As I caught a man's eye I would smile, but I had no idea what I was meant to say or do. After I don't know how long, I wondered what on earth I was doing. I felt like a prostitute, and yet I had no idea how to be one. Still feeling numb I walked out of the hotel and caught the train home. There is no doubt in my mind that if I had slept with someone that day, it could have led to a life of prostitution and worse. I said nothing to Pete, and the arguments over money continued.

Another close escape was after Pete and I split up

for the first time. I went on holiday to Spain with a girl I shared a house with. I didn't know her very well, but we booked a cheap package holiday. At the airport she got very drunk as she was terrified of flying. She was sick all the way to Spain, and when we got there she spent several days in bed recovering. I met Guy who was staying in our hotel with a friend. He certainly knew how to party which I loved. Every night we would go out after the others had gone to bed, and spend the nights dancing until morning. I hardly slept, and was having a great time.

The night before we were due to leave, Guy wanted us to spend the last night in a club. I was exhausted and had no idea how I was going to get through the night. Having told him this, he handed me a small white tablet, which he said would give me some energy. Again desperate to please I took it, and became uncontrollably high. I don't think I got off the dance floor all night. When Guy gave me a drink I couldn't put it to my mouth, and the drink went straight over my shoulder. I had no idea what was happening to me, but I loved it. Even now when I'm on a high I will dance to the radio, television adverts, and any music with a good beat. My mood becomes more and more elevated, believing I can do anything, even fly. Of course the only way is down.

The next morning in the hotel I was unable to relax, and my legs and arms were moving all the time. When we touched down back in England Guy realised the 'speed' he had given me was giving me serious side effects. Unsure what to do, he suggested I go back with him to his place. The friends picking him up thought he was mad. My friend was beside herself with worry, wondering what she would tell my parents if they phoned, which of course they did. I on the other hand didn't care where I went or what happened. I felt wonderful and yet very anxious and nauseous. I didn't know what to do to calm down.

Guy's house was incredible, set in lovely grounds, and he made me feel a million dollars. Having run me a bath, he wrapped me in a bath robe, gave me a back massage, and tried to help me relax, but to no avail. After several hours he put a line of 'coke' on top of the television, and encouraged me to snort it, saying it would help to calm me down. Not knowing what I was doing, and not really caring, I snorted the line of coke. I soon felt amazing, so relaxed and nothing seemed to matter.

I returned back home and to work, and for five days life was wonderful, but then suddenly I felt terribly depressed. It was on that day Guy telephoned, asking me to spend the weekend with him. I did spend several weekends with him, and a short holiday that ended up in disaster and finished our relationship. On several occasions I smoked cannabis with him, but I refused to have speed and coke again, realising this was a road I must not go down. Drugs affect people in very different ways, and there is no way of knowing what will happen. It is something I am not proud of, but it gave me an insight into how easy it can be to become hooked on drugs, and I'm not sure if this has contributed to my mental health problems.

Pete and I got back together, and bought a small flat on the south coast. His ex-wife had moved there with their daughter. Pete did not want to lose contact with her so I was happy to move with him. I also had too many bad memories of London, and hoped it would be a new start for both of us, but Pete's temper during this time did not improve. He had never got over his marriage breakdown, and although I knew she wouldn't take him back as he had had an affair with someone else, I felt terribly insecure as he spent more and more time with them. I was in a strange place, with no friends and I felt terribly lonely.

My periods suddenly stopped and I thought I might be pregnant. I was overjoyed believing we would now have a family. Pete was quiet all the way back to our flat, and when we got inside he became so angry. He told me that no one would have his baby apart from his ex-wife. I felt confused and devastated. I left the flat and walked round the village for hours. I had met only a handful of people, and had no idea where I was going to go. All I knew was I did not want to go back to the flat, I felt broken inside, and I hated him.

CHAPTER FOUR

The Glass Cracks, Shattering into Thousands of Pieces

Pete and I had met Catherine several weeks earlier in a pub. She had given me her address, and told me to pop round. As I knew no one in the area I turned up on her doorstep. She took me into her home, as she had done with many others. I never went back to the flat apart from to collect my things. It was during this time I started to experience lots of non-specific health problems. Pete had given me chlamydia after he had slept with an old girlfriend, and I had a lot of abdominal pain. I lost loads of weight, and when I was eventually admitted to hospital, Catherine was told I was dangerously dehydrated. Looking back I think I wanted to die. I was tired, weighed 7 stone, and had no fight left in me. When I was discharged I realised I somehow needed to change my life.

After all I had been through in London and West

Sussex, I moved to Lymington where Mum and Dad had retired. I dreaded moving in with them, but felt I had no choice. Catherine was really worried about me, and didn't feel she could give me the support I needed. The day my parents picked me up was hard for both of us. I had lived with her for over a year and had become very close to her. Catherine left early in the morning before they arrived, and it broke my heart moving away from her.

Not having love and affirmation from Mum, I had sought to find it from Catherine. She was unable to provide this, and it would have been wrong for her to try. I of course felt I was being abandoned again. I regret this was so hard for her. A feeling of abandonment in people that have been adopted is common. No one can make up for this devastating loss. When my parents arrived I shut myself firmly in my glass box trying to protect myself. As I got in the car I somehow managed to enter a new phase of my life. As I had done many times before, I pushed all the painful experiences and emotions somewhere inside me, as if nothing had happened. If there was a qualification for this, I would have been given a first class degree.

Now in Lymington I walked into my bedroom, and knew the only way to survive was to find a job and move out of home as quickly as possible. Mum and Dad continued to argue and I hated been drawn into it. On one occasion when my aunt and uncle visited, Mum became very angry. My aunt, very upset, left the bungalow, saying, 'Your mum looked at me as if she wanted me dead.' I told her she had looked at me that way countless times, since I had been adopted. She held me in her arms, unable to speak.

For as long as I could remember, I had wanted to be a nurse. If I could have started my training when I left school I would have, but I had no qualifications, and even though I successfully completed the nursery nursing course, I didn't meet the entry requirements I needed to start nursing. I decided to apply for an auxiliary nurse, now health care assistant, position, on a general ward at the local hospital.

From day one I loved every minute of it, more than I had enjoyed any other work. I was able to get a room in the hospital which got me out of living with Mum and Dad, and I gradually made friends in the area. From early on qualified staff were encouraging me to do my nurse training, something I didn't believe was achievable. Of course I had no qualifications other than my nursery nursing, but I decided to apply as a mature student, and was told I would need to sit a maths test. This filled me with dread, but I wanted to do this more than anything, and so Dad sat with me every night for months teaching me basic maths. I will always be grateful to him for that.

I sat the test, passed, and was accepted to train to become an enrolled nurse. This was a two-year course and I felt so proud to have been accepted. I enjoyed studying, working on wards, and being a student again. Living in halls of residence was fun, but I was more committed than ever to getting the balance right, between studying, working and partying. I still have the photograph of our group, in our uniforms, on my kitchen wall. I finally felt everything in my life was going well.

How wrong could I be? After months of life feeling wonderful, everything began to go wrong. After lifting a heavy patient whilst using the 'Australian Lift' (a procedure that is now banned), I hurt my back. After weeks of putting up with the pain, I talked to a doctor in my GP's practice. He advised me to give up nursing, as he believed I would struggle to work full-time on the wards. I was devastated, and could not believe what he was telling me. I again returned to Lymington, and left my nursing course.

Looking back it was the worse advice that I could have been given, and the Head of School told me later that had she not been away on leave, she would not have let me leave. The only way I could have returned was to apply again. As ours was the last year of training enrolled nurses I decided not to. Looking back, lifting was only part of the problem.

So much had happened in my life it was like I had a heavy weight constantly pulling me down. I would try so hard to achieve things, but would fall at the first post. Giving up on nursing just added to many other losses in my life. The loss of never knowing my birth parents, the loss of not having a loving, healthy relationship with my mother, the loss of trust that comes from being sexually abused, and now the loss of a career that I truly loved.

Determined not to stay in Lymington I moved back to Chichester. I rented a small cottage and worked in a day centre for people with learning difficulties. The assistant manager, Sam, asked me if I would go to a local church with him one Sunday. I had not been in a church for years, but agreed to go. Sam took me to a Christian camp called 'Spring Harvest'. I spent the whole week wondering what on earth it was all about. On the last night I went up for prayer. I don't remember what was said, but for the first time I felt an acceptance in my heart that I had not experienced before. Sam moved out of the area, but I continued going to the Anglican church. After a few months I was asked if I would do a 12-month course with the church, and was placed with a wonderful family. I lived with them for a number of years and it was during this time that I learnt what living in a loving family is all about. Despite being in my late twenties and early thirites I began to grow from a child into adulthood. I experienced a lot of pain in my back and legs, and due to mobility problems I spent some time in a wheelchair. It was during this time that I became very dependent on painkillers and muscle relaxants. For the family I lived with, having me in the family was at times very difficult and painful. I had so many emotional and physical needs. I will always be grateful for their love, kindness and patience, and for being the friends they are today. I love them dearly.

At another Christian camp, 'New Wine', I again was prayed for. As well as struggling to walk, my right hand had closed. I could not open my fingers, and I was having regular physiotherapy. As I was prayed for my fingers began to release one by one, and the sores on the palm of my hand disappeared. I remained in pain in my back and my legs, and continued using the wheelchair for some time. I don't fully understand why I was not totally healed at this time, but I knew God was looking after me. Gradually over the next few months the strength in my legs returned, and although I continued to live with the pain, I was now able to walk without any walking aid. I have gone on to experience the love of God many times in my life since then, and hope I always will.

Throughout my early years it was if I had lived my life on a stage. When people looked at me, they saw a caring individual who at times made stupid decisions, partied hard, but appeared cheerful most of the time, despite carrying the weight of the world on her shoulders. In my thirties and forties this weight brought me to my knees. Although I felt loved and accepted by the many friends I had made, I could no longer contain all the pain, fears, anxieties and hopelessness I felt. When Mum died in 1997 my world fell apart. I could no longer keep everything buried.

When she was alive I could not afford to be vulnerable. I used every ounce of strength I had to keep my life together. Once she had gone I had no reason to. All the fight went out of me and I finally collapsed. I am so grateful to the psychiatrist who my GP arranged for me to see in Chichester. He worked at The Priory, but saw a few NHS patients at the GP's surgery every week. At the end of the consultation he said he could not believe I had survived all I had been through without coming to the attention of the Mental Health Services.

Despite the hopelessness I felt, he helped me see I had inner strength which had brought me this far, and would see me through the coming years. I have held on to his words many, many times since then. After trying a few antidepressants the consultant prescribed Venlafaxine, an antidepressant, and Lithium, a mood stabiliser. After a few months I began to put my life back together. I had felt like a glass that had been dropped from a great height and was now in millions of pieces. Interestingly, I didn't feel abandoned by God. I have a very childlike faith, and whatever happens to me, I trust He is with me.

During our weekly, hour-long meetings, the psychiatrist helped me start putting my life back together. Prescribing medication was only a small part of what he did. He encouraged me to start telling my story to a counsellor, which I hadn't done before. I realised more than ever that I lived my life on a stage. Everyone saw Jane the dauntless, a girl who smiled at the outside world, but on the stage was a trap door. There was only so much that could be pushed under the floor: eventually the door sprung open and what spilled out was messy. It was like several jigsaws all mixed up together, and it made no sense.

The psychiatrist was also strict with me. I again had lost a great deal of weight, and he told me if I didn't start eating, I would quickly slide down a slippery slope into anorexia. This frightened me, because I hated being sick, and so I started to eat. He also encouraged me to take up some exercise, as this would help my mental health. I had enjoyed water aerobics several years earlier, but the thought of starting it now was too difficult to contemplate. He told me I would never feel like it, but to do it anyway, which I did. I continue to remember this sound advice daily.

I made life-long friends in Chichester who supported me through some very difficult times. After recovering from this first bout of depression I started to work part-time once again on general wards at the local hospital, as a health care assistant. Although I continued to have back pain, working on the wards was now easier, as we were not allowed to lift patients. As well as this I looked after two children who had lost their mother, picking them up from school, and staying with them until their dad got home.

Everything in my life seemed perfect, and this made the decision to leave the area very hard. I had visited a friend, a podiatrist, who was working for the

Leprosy Mission in Bangladesh. On another occasion we visited another friend, a physiotherapist, working in Sudan. I loved being in these Third World countries, and I had a desire to work in children's homes, or a pregnancy crisis counselling centre, in a developing country. I had completed a pregnancy crisis counselling course, and had helped at a local centre. I applied to a mission training college in Gloucester to complete a two-year diploma in theology, which included cultural studies.

Moving to Gloucester to study would mean I could learn about mission and different religions and cultures, and have the opportunity to do work experience both in this country and abroad. At the time I believed God was calling me to do it, but honestly I don't know. All through my life I would make sudden decisions to do things, often excitable and hyper.

This two-year diploma turned into three years, but didn't lead to me working abroad as I became reliant on the mental health services. I began a journey that took me through the darkest periods of my life, but also helped me to understand why I had made certain decisions in my life, and how my moods affected these decisions. It was a journey of self-discovery that was and still is at times very painful, but really understanding who I am has given me strength to carry on, and to hopefully encourage others who struggle with mental illness.

CHAPTER 5

Hospital

During the first year of college I struggled a great deal with unresolved personal issues in my life. I had had counselling in Chichester, from the psychiatrist and from a private counsellor. All of this had been positive that but I had had so much trauma and so many losses that whatever I did, they came back to haunt me. Attending lectures and writing assignments was incredibly hard. I put a great deal of pressure on myself trying to be a perfectionist. At school I hadn't cared about homework but as I got older, getting things right and getting good marks was very important to me. I only managed this with support from my tutor and a college counsellor.

I of course had a new GP in Gloucester, and as I appeared well I came off some of my psychotropic medication, including Lithium, which I had been on since 1997. Looking back I wished I had stayed on Lithium, as I felt very well whilst taking it, but it appeared to be the right thing to do at the time. As I approached the end of the first year, my mental health began to deteriorate. I couldn't concentrate on my work, or lectures. I either felt hyper or depressed. My GP arranged for me to see a community psychiatric nurse (CPN), which led me to attending a local day hospital for support.

Trying to finish the first year at college and attending anxiety management classes as well as creative writing, took its toll on me. I did complete that first year, but I ended up being admitted into a psychiatric hospital. I remember my first admission clearly. One of the nurses at the day hospital had called one of the doctors because of something I had written in the creative writing course. I can't remember any details, but I do remember feeling suicidal.

When the doctor said he felt it would be best if I was admitted into hospital as an informal patient, I felt numb and confused. How could this be happening to me? As an informal patient I could choose to leave hospital at any time, unless the nursing staff thought it was not in my best interest to leave. For some, doctors section, because when you are really unwell you can't always see what is best for you.

People are brought into hospital for assessment on a Section 2 under the Mental Health Act. An approved mental health professional (AMHP) will make the initial assessment, and it is necessary to be seen by two separate doctors. On admission you are given a patient rights leaflet, and have the right to appeal at a tribunal against the detention. This has to be made during the first 14 days that you are detained. During this time you have the right to refuse treatment. You can be detained for up to 28 days, and then an AMHP can assess you again for a Section 3, if it is felt necessary for your health. This can mean staying in hospital for up to six months, and then a year at a time. Many are admitted on an informal basis.

The thought of being admitted into a psychiatric hospital filled me with fear, and yet I felt relieved I didn't have to fight what I was feeling. Looking back I don't think I really wanted to die, I just wanted out. I wanted to get away from all the negative thoughts I was having, about my past, and life in general. I honestly believed the admission would only be for a few days, but I stayed in hospital for a total of three months.

Being in hospital was like being in another world. The building itself in some ways looked more like a hotel than a hospital. We all had our own room with en suite bathroom. There were day rooms, and we had three meals a day served to us. The support from the

doctors, nursing staff, care co-ordinators and coun-
sellors, and opportunities to attend classes such as
pottery and art, all help to get individuals back on
their feet as soon as possible. However, when there are
many people who are suffering from different mental
illnesses, the atmosphere is not always positive, and
staying too long in this atmosphere can make you
vulnerable to behavioural issues.

Seeing people kick off in the corridors or day areas
is difficult to watch. Sometimes televisions were
destroyed, and doors kicked in. People could be
restrained because of their behaviour, and it would
often take several staff to hold them down. I had
become so depressed I don't think I cared about what
was going on around me. I felt a horrible kind of
nothingness, and at times became almost catatonic,
where I found it hard to communicate, eat and sleep,
which made it hard for the consultant to treat me.

As I had moved to Gloucester, I did not have family
and old friends around me, and so the hospital had
very little idea of who I actually was. If there is one
thing I think the mental health service can improve
on is working with family and friends, often care
givers. This is sometimes difficult because service
users do not always give consent to talk to the people
around them, but I think single people are particu-

larly vulnerable if there is no one around to speak for them. Having said this, the mental health services are working hard to improve this, providing trained workers to work with carers, and of course advocacy groups.

Although Dad was still alive, and I had had very good friends for years, many of those lived 100 miles away. I had a lot of support from the college and new friends I had made, but they were unable to give a lot of information to the nurses. I think the hospital saw a very unwell woman, who had probably been like this for much of her life. I don't blame anyone for this.

I certainly was unwell, but I had functioned capably for most of my life. Mental health problems don't have to define you as a person. I had worked, studied, enjoyed travelling, being with friends, going to church, etc. All these helped to make me who I was. Having said this, when I look back there were many signs of mental illness in my early years. They had just not been picked up on. They say the average diagnosis for bipolar, for instance, is 10 years, as there have to be recurring manic episodes. I will talk about this more in later chapters.

The depression I felt was all consuming. It was like living in total blackness, and at first I couldn't see a way out, but slowly it began to lift. The groups I attended, and one-to-one sessions, helped me to build resilience. I think I had always had this as I had shown resilience many times during my life, but it is not always easy to see at the time. After three months in hospital I returned to Chichester and managed to get back on my feet. This was not easy to do. Even though I returned to my close friends, in hospital everything is done for you, and you become dependent on the staff and your surroundings. You want to leave, but it is a daunting prospect. After being discharged I didn't know what to do with myself, and the feelings of anxiety were hard to cope with. These days there are crisis teams to help with the transition, who will visit you daily if necessary to help you adjust to being out of hospital.

With love and care once again I got back on my feet, and the resilience I had was important, because it helped me overcome the challenges I had faced. It also helped me to become a stronger and wiser individual. It helped to build my self-esteem, which in turn helped me recognise what I had been able to achieve. Returning to college was important to me, as I had not completed a lot in my life, and I wanted to complete the diploma even if I couldn't work abroad following the completion of the course, and so I returned to Gloucester.

During the second year, the personal development tutor/counsellor arranged for me to meet with a mission counsellor in London, to see if it was wise for me to work abroad. After a long interview, I was devastated to hear it would not be advisable for me to move and work in another country. Although my dreams were shattered I respected her honesty, and could see that moving brings so many losses. Losses of family and friends being close by, the loss of culture, and not knowing if good health care would be adequate were all reasons why it would have been unwise to choose the career I had planned.

Although I was coping with lectures and assignments, I was again experiencing breakthrough symptoms of sometimes feeling hyper and other times feeling depressed. Coming to college in the first place, moving to a new city, and planning to live in a Third World country, were all part of me becoming hyper. I would make sudden decisions and have grandiose ideas, which can all be signs of mania. I will talk about this in later chapters, but once again, as I look back, I can see this has happened many times during my life.

I somehow got through to graduation day, which was one of the happiest and saddest days of my life. I felt I had achieved a lot, and graduating with my friends, as all students know, meant a great deal, but seeing many of them go on to work in different countries when I couldn't go, was also devastating. I guess many students feel the same now, not being able to get the jobs or careers they set out enthusiastically to get. I had just about managed to complete the course, with the support of the college and the mental health services, but it was such a struggle.

Giving up my dream and instead attending the local day hospital, my mental health declined. The college kindly let me stay in my room for a while, and then my very close friends from Chichester bought a house for me to rent in Gloucester. Over the next couple of years I had several shorter admissions into hospital, and it seemed impossible for me to find any way out of this cycle. On several occasions I took overdoses, which again was more about me wanting to find a way out rather than actually wanting to die.

I also began to self-harm in other ways. For me this was cutting my arms. I now wish I hadn't done this, as I am left with permanent scars, but at the time I didn't care what I looked like. It is hard to explain why I felt I needed to, but the pain inside was so great, and I didn't know how to express it. When I cut my arms and felt physical pain it felt like a release, a release of anxiety and pain. It was a coping strategy, but not a positive one. Talking about anxieties and pain inside is a much better coping strategy, and there are other physical things you can do, such as holding on to ice cubes.

I remember one meeting I had with one of the psychiatric doctors and my care co-ordinator after a fairly feeble overdose attempt. The doctor asked me, 'Jane, where do we go from here?' I left the room wondering if I was about to be abandoned by the service I had become so dependent on. I was later told this would not have happened, but it had a profound effect on me. The following morning, I woke up early and clearly saw two roads ahead of me. One continued on the road I was on, attending the day hospital every day, and continuing to self-harm, which might have easily led to me taking my own life; or I could take the other road, and somehow find the strength to move on from this devastating depression, and hopefully into some kind of work.

I shocked my care co-ordinator the next day by saying I needed help to move on and would he help me. I am so thankful to him for the support he gave me. He is a great nurse, and I know many have gone on to be helped by him. Doctors, nurses and other psychiatric staff give so much to the people they work with, and I would like to thank everyone who has given and continues to give so much to myself and others who live with mental illness.

CHAPTER 6

Putting up Scaffolding

After spending a short time at a rehabilitation centre in Birmingham I returned to Gloucester not really knowing what was ahead of me, but I felt more hopeful. I had stopped self-harming, and was keen to find some voluntary work. I approached the college where I had been studying. They gave me some work in the general office, doing some basic administration. This gave me the confidence and the time I needed to look at other opportunities.

At the same time the day hospital where I had attended so many courses, such as anxiety management, asked if I would be prepared to help out with some of the courses. I felt privileged to have been asked, and I was paid a small amount of money for helping. Having been on various benefits for so long, it was hard to make the transition from being dependent on income support and disability living allowance to earning a wage.

The system is once again changing, but at the time I was able to earn so much, and keep my benefits, receive a rent allowance, and to be exempt from council tax. This was important, as I could not have moved from not working for so long to working full-time. It is not an easy step to make, and I think it puts a lot of people off making the decision to return to work. I can only say, I found the job centre and other agencies such as citizens advice very helpful.

I remember at the time there was building work going on at the back of my house. From my living room window I could see the flats being built. As they completed one level, they put up scaffolding to complete the next. For me this mirrored what was happening to me. I would complete one level, before moving onto the next. By the time the builders completed one floor, and put up more scaffolding, I was ready to start another stage in my life. It was a cathartic experience.

I was able to start earning a small amount from the college, and also from the mental health services. At the same time I contacted a local counselling service and arranged to see a cognitive behavioural therapist. Using cognitive behavioural therapy (CBT), I was able to start understanding myself better than I had before.

I'm not sure I could have coped with this sort of therapy before I had talked through the traumas I had been through. It involves not only talking about past issues, but also doing a lot of homework to try and change negative thought processes. When I began to do this, CBT helped me to change the way I think, feel and behave.

This particular kind of therapy helps individuals to look at their patterns of limited thinking. For instance I was very good at overgeneralisation, expressing statements such as, 'Nobody loves me,' or 'This always happens to me.' Of course there are people who love me, and things don't always happen to me, but it is very easy to overgeneralise. I am also good at mind reading, where I make sudden judgements about people.

An example of this is if you see someone you know across the road, and you're sure they have seen you, but they don't acknowledge you. It is easy to make a judgement that they are ignoring you, that you must have done something wrong. In reality they may not have seen you, or they may have been preoccupied.

It is easy to ruminate on these things and then to get depressed by negative thoughts. I can look back and see I was mind reading even as a child, trying to read Mum's mind, especially when she looked at me in such a way that I believed she wanted me dead.

These thoughts had rooted themselves deep within me.

I was also good at catastrophising, where I would always see the negative in everything. Actually the list was endless. Over weeks and months I worked hard to challenge my negative thinking. The counsellor encouraged me to keep a thought journal where I would challenge my automatic thoughts such as 'I'm no good,' 'I don't think I can go on,' and 'I'm so worthless.' I had many of these automatic thoughts that were like a noose around my neck dragging me down.

In one session with one particular counsellor she asked me to imagine myself standing on a station platform. She said she could see me struggling to carry very heavy suitcases. Each of the cases contained a different trauma – abuse, anxieties and so on – that was weighing me down. She encouraged me to draw a picture of myself, and to add suitcases, writing on each one the many things that were making me anxious. I lost count of how many there were. After this the counsellor asked me to close my eyes, to imagine trying to carry all the cases at once, and then to let them go, walking away and leaving them where they were.

The idea was not to walk away and not pick any of

them up again, that would be impossible, but to pick one up at a time, to open it, look inside, and deal with whatever the anxiety or problem was. I have done this many, many times since that day, as I am quick to try to pick them all up. The release you feel when you drop the cases is immense, and I have encouraged others to use this exercise many times since then.

I was also very good, as are others, at saying 'I should do this,' or 'I must do that.' Changing 'I must do that,' to 'I wonder if I can do this today,' takes a lot of pressure off you. I wrote out flash cards at the time and put them around the house. Some of these were:

'I'm doing what I can right now.'

'I can turn my day around.'

'My attitude if positive will turn my day around.'

'I've got through this before, and I will again.'

'I do have problems, but I'm working on them.'

I have included some of these in my early warning signs, which I have included in a later chapter.

Trying to stick to these and others was not easy, in fact it was hard work, but the more I read them, and completed the exercises the CBT counsellor set me, the more I believed in myself. If an event happened such as having an argument with my husband over not completing a task, I would automatically have negative thoughts, such as, 'He doesn't understand, therefore he doesn't care.' This would spiral into such thoughts as 'This is the end.' I would then feel anxiety, depression, hopelessness, and so on.

Events lead to thoughts, and then to feelings. If you can change the thought, you can change the feeling. If I had thought, 'I can take time to explain why I didn't complete the task', I would not have had such devastating feelings. I had many negative thoughts which pulled me down, which meant as I got older I continually struggled with a low mood and anxiety. Working on uncovering my automatic thoughts helped to reduce my anxieties, hopelessness and depression.

As well as my thoughts and feelings I was fighting the effects of what is thought to be a chemical imbalance. In Joseph Carver's article on the internet he writes:

When patients talked about their past this led founders of psychology and psychiatry to believe that issues that began in childhood caused many mental health problems. But questions were still not answered. It became clear that many mental health problems also had a physical component. The picture became easier to understand when chemicals in the brain called neurotransmitters were discovered. These neurotransmitters, including a chemical Serotonin, can affect our sleep, and be related to depression and to a variety of mental

∞∽∞

health conditions such as anorexia and obsessive-compulsive disorder.

As research in neurotransmitters continued, studies between neurotransmitters and mental health conditions revealed a strong connection between amounts of certain neurotransmitters in the brain and the presence of specific psychiatric conditions. Neurological research has identified over fifty (50) neurotransmitters in the brain. Research also tells us that several neurotransmitters are related to mental health problems – Dopamine, Serotonin, Norepinephrine, and GABA (Gammo Aminobutyric Acid).

Too much or too little of these neurotransmitters are now felt to produce psychiatric conditions such as schizophrenia, depression, bipolar affective disorder, obsessive-compulsive disorder, and ADHD. [...] The key is looking for those symptoms that are known to be related to chemical changes in the brain.

Carver, Joseph, M. PhD (10 August 2011)

I am not an expert in any way about the different mental health conditions, but I do know consultants carefully take time in diagnosing different illnesses. Getting medications right is not easy, and taking medication has been such a big part of my life for so long. As well as taking psychotropic medication, I have continued to take a lot of painkillers. This has meant I have taken up to 25 tablets a day, which is constantly reviewed. Many of these bring different side effects which are unpleasant. I have no choice but to persevere while the doctors get the right balance. This is the same for many people with different conditions.

CHAPTER 7

My Rock

As the scaffolding neared completion at the back of my flat I was now in a relationship with Mike. We had met during my last admission to hospital. Mike would pick me up and take me out most days. This means a lot when you are in hospital. He became and still is my rock. I eventually moved in with him and continued to work part-time for the mental health services. Unbelievably at the same time, my dad met my stepmum, and it was wonderful to see them married in their eighties.

It was at this time that the mental health services made radical changes. The day hospital closed and individuals were encouraged to get involved in more community activities, therefore promoting inclusion. For a few this has been beneficial, and led to them joining local recreational centres and attending colleges. But for many it has led to individuals being more isolated. They find it too difficult to socialise with others and therefore need more support from different mental health teams.

Having moved in with Mike I felt more secure than I had done for many years. This enabled me to be more confident and I applied for a full-time job with one of the mental health teams. I was incredibly proud of myself for getting the job, and for all I had achieved, especially as I had been unwell for so many years. The step up to working full-time was hard, and at times incredibly tiring, but it was a privilege to help others who experience similar problems and challenges that I battle with.

Taking advice from some of my colleagues, I chose to selectively share some of the mental health challenges I have experienced with a few service users I worked with. It would not be professional to share how I'm feeling, or to say statements such as, 'I know how you feel,' but being open when appropriate has hopefully helped to encourage some of the people I worked with.

Thankfully mental illness is talked about a lot more in the media, highlighted by mental health awareness weeks, and 'Time to Change' is England's biggest ever attempt to end stigma and discrimination that face people with mental health problems. It is a campaign to change attitudes, and behaviour too. One in four of us will experience a mental health problem in our lifetime and, if we do, we are highly likely to face stigma and discrimination from others.

As well as having its own website and holding mental health awareness days in the community Time to Change can also be accessed on Facebook, YouTube and on Twitter. Celebrities such as Ruby Wax have pledged, '... *to talk openly about my mental illness and to help get people talking about the 'M' word.*' Stephen Fry speaks out '... *to fight stigma and to give a clearer picture of mental illness that most of us know little about.*' Frank Bruno writes, '*If there is one thing I've learned from my illness it is that there is no shame and no harm in saying you need help. Mental illness can happen to anyone. You can be a dustman, a politician, a Tesco worker, anyone. It could be your dad, your brother or your aunt. People need to have compassion for others.*'

The group 'The Wanted' wrote:

People with mental health problems face prejudice every day. It's the small things we all say and do without meaning to, that cause the most harm – like telling someone to 'snap out of it' or not keeping in touch. We're supporting Time for Change, to help show that we can all make a small change that will make a big difference.

Time to Change, 2008. Funded by the
Department of Health

∞◡∞

There are many others who contribute to this site, and the Time to Change campaign.

Bipolar UK is another charity that is dedicated to supporting individuals who struggle daily with this devastating illness. They provide a quarterly magazine called *Pendulum* that includes articles on subjects like nutrition and mood, link mentoring and advice on benefits as well as letters from people living with bipolar. They are also involved in research and provide support groups around the country not only for those who have bipolar, but also for families and carers.

I have found that once I explain what mental illness is like for me, people are generally very accepting. When I'm depressed I don't want people to fuss around me. Friends visit, take me out for coffee, and even cook for me, but they don't expect me to talk. Every day feels like walking through treacle. Simple tasks, such as washing my hair, are hard to achieve. I try to keep a routine, such as eating regularly, even if I don't feel like it; for instance going to bed at the same time every night, even if I can't sleep and end up getting up in the middle of the night. A lot of this book was written between 2 and 5am when I was high!

I try to get regular exercise, and generally keep things as normal as possible. The temptation is to go to bed and stay there, hiding away from everyone. I know some people who have to do this, but for me it doesn't work. I need to be disciplined and thankfully Mike tries to help me with this. I know it is incredibly hard for him to see me so low, when I want to hide away, and equally frustrating when I am high, wanting to play music loud and dance. He finds the highs harder to cope with than the lows. I guess I am more unpredictable. We are both thankful to our wonderful family and friends, as well as the mental health services that support us.

CHAPTER 8

Learning to Live with Bipolar

Within months of my starting my new job, my dad had a serious car accident. Mike and I spent a lot of time travelling up and down the motorway, visiting him in hospital, and staying with my stepmum. Despite being discharged from hospital, Dad did not recover well in and in four months he had died. I was devastated. Although I now had Mike, Dad and I were incredibly close, especially after all we had been through together.

This also meant I had a lot of time off work. Shortly after dad died I started a course in mental health, hopefully leading to a qualification as an Associate Practitioner. I didn't feel I could cope with studying for three years to become a mental health nurse, but felt studying for a year would be achievable. So I desperately wanted to succeed in this, especially as I had had to give up on other courses in the past.

The course was split between studying one day at

university, two days' work experience and two days in my usual job. There was of course work to do at home. Although I tried really hard to meet all the targets required, frustratingly my mental health began to suffer. As well as grieving for my dad, I soon became depressed and was unable to continuing studying. I had three months off work and when I returned I cut my hours to 30 a week.

It was during this time that I probably learnt the most about my illness. I know I'm an intelligent person who is more than capable of gaining a qualification, but having a mental illness makes it difficult for me to achieve all that I want to. Any pressure, trauma or change can be a trigger for me either to have a 'high' or a 'low'. In fact there does not always appear to be a trigger for a relapse.

During the years I have received a diagnosis of Bipolar Affective Disorder. The Royal College of Psychiatrists' website explains this as:

'Bipolar disorder is a condition in which a young person has extreme changes in mood – periods of being unusually happy (known as mania or hypomania), and periods of being unusually sad (depression). It is sometimes called manic depressive disorder or bipolar mood disorder.

The mood swings are way beyond what would be considered 'normal' for a particular individual, and are out of keeping with their usual behaviour. Bipolar disorder in younger people is extremely rare. It is much more like to occur and be identified in young people during their teenage years. In adults it affects 1 in 100 people.

Although the causes are not fully understood, bipolar disorder tends to run in families. Episodes can be triggered by physical illness, stressful events or lack of sleep. In bipolar a person can have manic or hypo manic periods (or episodes) which can come on quite rapidly and last for one week or longer. Depressive periods lasting at least 2 weeks, mixed periods of the above. Hypomania is a milder form of mania (less severe and for shorter periods). However, if left untreated, it can become more severe, and may be followed by an episode of depression.

Royal College of Psychiatrists (2011)

Receiving a diagnosis has helped me to understand why I have so many rapid mood swings. When I'm high I want to listen to loud music with a beat. To dance, clap, sing, laugh and dance to Zumba on the Wi console feels fantastic. I become very talkative and find it hard to stop, often referred to as rapid speech. It is like being propelled into the air at fast speed, or taking a drug, like a stimulant. You want more and more.

Life seems great. I believe I can achieve anything, and often become creative. I guess that is why I've been able to write this book. After a while however, words, ideas and thoughts become too fast. I'm unable to slow down, both physically and in my head. Nothing makes sense, and I'm unable to hang on to any one thought at a time. My memory goes blank, and I find it difficult to remember one thing to the next. Getting older doesn't help this!

In many ways I am unable to make sense of anything. I want to drive the car fast, and feel as if the car is going to take off. At these times I can become reckless, leading me so far to only having minor scrapes, but concerning enough for Mike to take my car keys off me, despite my protests. The highs are amazing feelings until it is impossible to think about anything clearly any more. I'm unable to shut off, and don't want to sleep.

My long-suffering husband spends many a night trying desperately to get back to sleep. During this time I need mood-stabilisers and anti-psychotics. They help to calm everything down, but are not always easy to tolerate with the side-effects such as constipation. The temptation is not to take anything, but it is important to listen to the psychiatric team, even when you don't want to, which is hard to do when you are on a high.

Although the highs are great, they are usually followed by the lows. For me this is like free-falling down a deep well into the dark. There appears no way out, and all you can see is a faint light somewhere in the distance, but you can find no way out. During these times death feels preferable, but I don't have the energy to do anything about it. I would also not want to hurt Mike, all the family and our wonderful friends.

However, the feelings are very real. I feel incredibly lonely, despite having wonderful people around me. I can only hang on to the fact that I've been here before, and I will finally come out the other side. Often climbing out of this dark depression is like climbing one ledge at a time, literally hanging on by my fingers. It can be a very slow process. At other times it is like being propelled out of it at a very fast rate, once again feeling hypo manic. This is often known as rapid-cycling, and is not easy to cope with. I can end up feeling high and low all at the same time. Again I'm reliant on the expertise of the psychiatrist, and the support of all the team.

Taking medication is different for everyone and does not appear to always be an exact science, but the psychiatrist takes time, not only making the right diagnosis, but also looking into the right medication, and the contraindications with other medications. I find being in a mixed state especially hard to cope with. It is like being an elastic band, being pulled one way, and then another. I end up feeling very agitated and anxious which is probably the worst part of the illness.

I am too agitated to sit, lie down, or to stand up. I want to keep moving, but my legs and back hurt so much and I've no idea what to do with myself. I again have to hang on to the fact that I will come through it. It takes every ounce of strength to try to relax and not to give in to the feeling of 'I don't want to go on'.

This was particularly hard in 2011–2012. I began struggling at work, feeling stressed about everything I did. This was followed by me starting to feel hyper. My driving began to suffer, as did everyday tasks. I was referred to the occupational doctor at work, and was told to take time off work. This was followed by months of feeling high. I loved it, even thrived on it, but I soon became reckless, leaving the house and not telling people where I was going, not looking for traffic when crossing the roads, driving fast to loud music, spending money, staying up all night, and behaving oddly for no reason. I had to send my driving licence back to the DVLA, and it took months for me to get it back again. Thankfully I was entitled to a bus pass whilst I was unable to drive.

I spent months trying several medications, and found it hard to tolerate them. Eventually my thoughts wouldn't stop racing, and I couldn't make sense of anything. I spent a week in hospital, and came home under the care of the crisis team. Not long after this the inevitable depression kicked in. I became withdrawn, exhausted, felt paranoid when I went out, struggled with anxiety, and was consumed with feelings of death. I was now taking around 25 tablets a day, including the painkillers. This was the only time I really wondered if God existed. I felt no relief and no peace. Having now been off work a year, I lost my job which I had fought so hard to get. I was devastated.

After a meeting with occupational health I had arranged to meet a friend at her house. On the way I had to cross a train line. I had to wait a while as two or three trains were coming. As I stood there my heart raced, as I considered running out in front of a train. It was probably the first time I really wanted to die. The thought of Mike being visited by the police, to tell him what I had done, made me telephone the crisis team, and my care co-ordinator. They were able to give me the support I needed to go on to meet my friend. It was a frightening experience.

Eventually the depression and anxiety began to fade, and I started to get my life back on track. I applied to a nursing agency and I am now working one or two days a week, usually in nursing homes. It feels great to be working again. Within a few months I have reduced my medication, and am now taking only eight tablets a day. My goal is to reduce this further over the next few weeks, and not to take any painkillers. I still have back pain, but I am determined to try to cope with this in a different way, such as using exercise and stretches to relieve it. I have been taking painkillers for around 20 years, and it is easy to become dependent on them. I honestly believed I couldn't live without them, but this clearly is not true.

If I'm honest there are breakthrough symptoms, where at times I am feeling hyper. I am only taking one psychotropic medication which helps calm me down, but I am taking a very low dose. The psychiatric team want me to increase this, but when you are feeling hyper it is hard to agree to what they are saying. One way to help with this is to write down your early warning signs, and to make an action plan for each stage. It took me some time to write this, but I hope it might be helpful to others to me to include this in the next chapter.

CHAPTER 9

Early Warning Signs

MARCH 2013

Depression: Early Phase - can go from high to depression in one day (Rapid Cycling)

- Feeling dissatisfied with me. Everything I do does not seem good enough. Tend to judge self and consider how others might be judging me.

- Starting to feel hopeless and helpless.

- Feel that I am losing control of everything that's going on around me.

- Having difficulty concentrating on anything. e.g. reading or watching television. Don't seem to be able to follow conversations as well. This may well be due to being preoccupied with random things, whatever is happening.

- Feeling depressed or low in mood. See self at the top of the well, there are ledges and if I slip down onto one or two ledges it's OK. If I go into free fall then I will keep going down till I hit rock bottom and there is nothing I can do to stop it.

- Feeling very quiet, running out of energy both emotionally and physically. Feeling very tired and lacking energy to enable me to be bothered with anything. It becomes hard to do the basics.

- Feel unable to cope, to manage everyday tasks, e.g. planning and cooking meals or doing household jobs like the washing.

- Feeling tense and anxious. Anxiety will be there from the moment of waking, and comes 'like a bolt'.

- Sometimes aware of my heart racing, muscular tension and various aches and pains.

- Starting to have thoughts generally about death, and about me dying.

Action plan for 'depression' - early phase

- Challenge negative thinking, e.g. 'All or nothing thinking' – Why do I think everyone is talking about me? Or 'Everything I do goes wrong'.

What evidence do I have for it? It can't be true that everyone is talking about me, and not everything I do goes wrong! In the same way challenge why I think I'm not good enough.

- Challenge myself about 'mind reading', e.g. 'I know they don't like me'. I don't know this at all. I cannot read minds. Check out negative thinking with family and friends.

- Challenge the 'should, ought and must': I must get this done, or I should be the best; I can only do what I can do!

- Challenge thinking the worst, e.g. 'Mike hasn't called, he must have had an accident.' He might have forgotten his phone, or just be busy at work.

- Think about ways I can relax, e.g. finding a peaceful environment, maybe in the living room with the wood burner on, listening to relaxing music, and if anxious think about my breathing, using mindfulness techniques.

- 'Mindfulness walking' – go for a walk and listen to what is going on around me, including the birds, the wind, cars, people, and other sounds I can hear. What does the ground feel like under my feet, what can I smell, do I feel hot or cold? Bring my thoughts back to the here and now.

• Look at why I'm feeling anxious and low. Am I doing too much? Try to calm things down. Be honest about how much I'm doing by myself and with others.

• Let others know how I'm feeling, e.g. anxious, low, quiet, stressed, experiencing negative thoughts and wanting to withdraw from others, and let work know if things are getting too much for me.

Depression: Middle Phase

• Feeling very quiet and withdrawn. Finding it hard to communicate. Wanting to lie on the sofa and do nothing. Find it hard to make eye contact.

• Don't feel like eating. Can't decide what to eat or to cook. Feel like I've lost the ability to cook. Generally have no interest in food.

• Having no interest in things. Really no or poor concentration. Unable to motivate myself.

Starting not to care about anything. Stare at the television but can't take anything in.

- Feeling useless or helpless and very tired. Finding it hard to do the simplest of tasks.

- Having aches and pains, especially in my back and legs.

- Hopelessness feelings getting worse. Feel like I've slipped further down the well, almost to the bottom.

- Having more thoughts about dying. Feel like driving fast and letting the steering wheel go so that the car crashes ending everything.

Action plan for 'depression' - middle phase

- Talk to Mike, close friends, CPN or consultant about feeling quiet, withdrawn, and finding it hard to communicate.

- If I can, continue to challenge negative thinking as in action plan for early phase, and check thinking out with others.

- Find reasons to get out of the house, e.g. meeting a friend for coffee.

- Be honest about wanting to die, but remember that these feelings do pass, and it is likely I don't really want to die, I just want the feelings to go away. I have got through this before, and I can get through it again!

- Give car keys to Mike so that I can't drive, putting myself and others in danger.

- Do simple tasks that I can concentrate on, e.g. making some cards, cooking simple meals, meeting friends for coffee and going for short walks.

- Generally look after myself. Eat well, try to relax and be kind to myself.

- Look at taking some time off work.

- Discuss medication with professionals.

Depression: Late Phase

- Feel like everything's stopped. Finding it hard to function. Dropped to the bottom of the well. Everything is dark, and I don't have the strength to pick myself up.

- My movements seem slow, and I feel like I am dragging myself round. Feel exhausted. It is too tiring even to talk. Find it almost impossible to make eye contact. Can become catatonic.

- Nothing matters any more. Consumed with thoughts about dying. Have thought about taking overdoses, and have done in the past. Have thought about jumping out in front of a train. Feel that death would be a relief.

- Feel like I'm being watched, paranoid, particularly when I'm in the supermarket. Feel like cameras or people are watching me in case I steal something.

- Feel forgetful or 'far away'. No concentration. Barely existing.

- In later stage of late phase, feel tense, afraid or anxious. Find it really hard to leave the house. Wake up feeling very anxious.

- Feel irritable or quick tempered.

Action plan for 'depression' - late phase

- Only do the very basics, making sure I get up, have a shower, and try to eat a fairly good diet.

- Try to communicate that I need help with everyday tasks, e.g. shopping, cooking and cleaning.

- Get plenty of rest and try to arrange visits from friends for short periods.

- Take time off work. I'm not a failure, this is just how it is, but I can get through it. I have found the inner strength to get through it before and I will again.

- Try to communicate any negative thoughts, such as wanting to harm myself, with the right people, e.g. Mike and the professionals. Challenge thoughts that I'm being watched in the supermarket. I'm not a mind reader, I can't possibly know people are talking about me or watching me.

- Be honest about the support I feel I need from the professionals, e.g. number of visits from CPN, crisis intervention and maybe a stay in hospital. Listen to what the professionals say they believe I need, and accept what they say.

- Remember I can get through this. The depression and anxiety does pass.

- Discuss medication/treatment with professionals.

- Look at risk management, e.g. spending time in a safe environment. This might be at home with professionals and friends dropping in for regular short visits. Don't put myself in risky situations, e.g. going to train line as I have before. If I find myself in these situations, remember I can call Mike, friends or professionals. I have been here before and got through it, and I can get through it again. Things will get better. I need to be patient.

Highs: Early Phase

- Feel very talkative and outgoing. Everything feels great. Feel like I can't stop talking.

- Feel like sorting through everything, and throwing loads away.

- Feel very confident and extremely happy. Lots of things seem funny. Start to feel I can achieve anything.

- Feel like skipping, clapping, being silly. Don't want to sit down, sitting is boring.

- Feel very excited. Everything feels great. Don't want it to stop – love it!

- Sleep becomes restless or unsettled.

- Have difficulty concentrating. Mind/thoughts beginning to race, and starting to become preoccupied.

- Start to feel I want to drive fast with the music loud, manage not to do it.

- Start writing more of my book, and looking into getting it published.

- Start drinking coffee – feel like I need the caffeine, like a drug.

Action plan for 'highs' – early phase

- Be honest about how I'm feeling with myself, Mike, friends and professionals, e.g. GP, CPN or consultant.

- Notice I'm more talkative, wanting to dance to loud music with a beat, especially the *Latino Summer* CD.

- Notice I want to start doing more to my book, and get it published, and that I believe I can achieve anything. Stay in the here and now, and don't pursue grandiose ideas.

- Notice I'm finding everything funny, excitable, and calm everything down, e.g. spending time in a calm environment, perhaps listening to quieter music, or go for a walk, which might help to get rid of some of the energy I have. Listen to when I say 'everything's cool' constantly both in my head and to others.

- Do quieter activities, e.g. making cards instead of charging around. If I go for a walk, walk at a steady pace, instead of walking fast.

- Get regular sleep and meals, don't drink too much tea and don't drink coffee. If I don't want to go to bed at night, make sure I do go at regular times.

- Talk to professionals re change in medication. Listen to their advice, taking more medication if they advise this. Take the medication at night as it helps me calm down and go to sleep.

- Look at how many shifts I'm working, and work fewer shifts so I'm not too busy as this fuels the highs.

- It is important to calm things down now, because it gets out of control quickly, moving to the middle and late phases, which are harder to control. Remember, this is then followed with depression.

Highs: Middle Phase (Move into this phase fairly fast)

- Feel like I can't sit still. Wanting to dance all the time to loud and fast music. Have no physical pain.

- Love the high and don't want it to stop.

- Start driving fast, loving it, listening to loud music. Want to drive and drive and drive. It feels great.

- Want to walk and walk, not telling people where I'm going. Am told I walk across roads without looking out for vehicles, cyclists, etc.

- Feel very energetic, needing little sleep. Can stay up all night and all the next day.

- New ideas are constantly coming into my head. I can achieve or be anything, e.g. be on and win *X Factor*, be an air hostess, or anything really.

- Behave oddly for no reason, e.g. laughing or talking to myself. Everything feels so funny and great. Feel like being open re sexual matters.

- Feel as if my thoughts might not be my own. Thoughts starting to race more, not making any sense.

- Feel like playing tricks or being generally silly. Life really is so funny.

- Have the urge to spend lots of money on clothes, suddenly booking concerts or a holiday, etc.

- Feel more and more confused about things, and can't concentrate on anything, e.g. what I'm watching on television.

Action plan for 'highs' - middle phase

- Again be honest about how I'm feeling, e.g. wanting to dance more or work lots. Calm things down and pay attention to my environment, and be honest about how I'm feeling. Ask others for help to calm things down.

- Challenge my thinking, i.e. 'My thoughts are not my own', of course they are. I must try to stay calm, and ground myself in the here and now, e.g. mindful walking/breathing.

- Don't drive fast or listen to loud music. Hand my car keys to Mike, especially when I want to take off, not letting others know where I'm going.

- Don't spend too much money, book holidays or concerts on line, and give Mike my bank card to look after if I can't control what I'm spending.

- Look at risk management, making sure I stay safe, especially when I'm out and not concentrating where I'm going. Take extra care when crossing roads, as I will often not look where I'm going.

- Tell Mike and others where I'm going, and for how long.

- Discuss medication changes with professionals and listen to their advice.

- Calm everything down and don't work too hard. Discuss having some time off work with the Agency, Mike, and professionals, e.g. CPN or GP.

- Get regular sleep, going to bed at sensible times, not staying up all night. Eat sensible diet and again, don't drink too much tea or coffee.

Highs: Late Phase

- Dancing more and more to loud music, and generally cannot stop moving. Legs and back beginning to ache because I can't stop.

- Starting to feel very agitated and as if I could lose my temper.

- Feel like I'm driving on a race track whilst listening to loud music. Want to disappear whilst driving, not letting anyone know where I'm going. Feel like I'm going to make stupid decisions. Feel like I'm going to drive faster and faster and then let go of the steering wheel and let the car fly.

- Want to go walking in the middle of the night, and don't think about the risks.

- Am told I become more unpredictable.

- Thoughts won't stop racing. Can't make sense of anything. Starts to be frightening. Feel like thoughts might be controlled.

- Others have difficulty following what I'm saying.

- Want it all stop but don't know how, which makes me feel anxious. At same time I still want to be high.

- My speech becomes jumbled or is full of odd words.

- Feeing assertive, wanting to tell people what to do.

- Sometimes I feel I'm not real.

- Feel like being more explicit about sexual matters.

- As thoughts race, find it more difficult to cope and manage everyday tasks.

Action plan for 'highs' – late phase

- Look at risk management, thinking about a safe environment, e.g. at home or with friends, trying to keep everything calm, e.g. listening to relaxing music, or doing a calm craft activity such as making cards.

- Talk to professionals, e.g. GP, CPN or consultant about how I'm feeling, especially when I feel I can't stop moving.

- Listen carefully to advice about medication and follow it.

- Take time off work and try to relax.

- Stay safe, letting others know where I am going, and for how long.

- Don't play loud/fast music.

- Talk to Mike and professionals about the anxiety I feel, especially feeling I can't stop or calm down, and my heart racing. Remember this does pass, and if I follow their advice carefully I can calm down.

- Don't drive! Give my keys to Mike. If I can't do this, Mike to take my keys off me. Give house keys to Mike if I am up all night, so that I can't go for a walk in the middle of the night, putting myself in danger.

- Discuss regular visits from CPN or crisis team intervention, and possibly short stay in hospital, but remember I have got through this before and I can get through it again.

Obviously these are personal to me, but they are a useful tool, and widely used by the mental health services. The action plans are important, as they hopefully keep you well.

Epilogue

For me, bipolar is like two sides of a coin. In many ways it is a cruel illness, as of course are many other illnesses. When you are depressed, the feelings of hopelessness are unbearable. The other side of the coin is a lot more exciting. When you are high there is nothing like it. You feel so creative, and life seems great. You can achieve anything, climb a mountain, or swim the channel.

These highs don't last though, and the lows are hard to bear. There are times in between when I am very well. Whilst writing this I feel as though I'm in a mixed state, where I can feel hyper, OK, and low, all in the same day. Mostly I feel great. It is the time when I should take notice of the early warning signs, but for some reason this is sometimes hard to do. This is why you should get people close to you to point things out, and sometimes be assertive.

So would I be without bipolar? The truth is I don't know. Certainly when I'm high, I would answer 'no', but when I'm depressed, I would do anything for it to go. Last year I reached 50 and it was great to celebrate it with family and friends. I don't think I believed I would get this far, but with determination and resilience, I am still here today. My faith has played a big part in that too, and I am thankful that God has seen me through some very difficult times.

I hope this book has given an insight into what it is like living with a mental illness. I started off by saying I am in no way unique. There are many who struggle daily, and often a lot more than I do. Living in my glass box is challenging, with many highs and lows, but it is part of me, and I'm proud to have got this far. I am also proud of everyone who struggles with mental illness of many different types. This book is for you!

Lightning Source UK Ltd.
Milton Keynes UK
UKOW03f1435260314

228872UK00001B/7/P